TRIPLE MEASURES

Other Works by K.M.Miller, Ian Gouge, Tom Furniss

Novels and Novellas

The Opposite of Remembering - Ian Gouge, Coverstory books, 2020
At Maunston Quay - Ian Gouge, Coverstory books, 2019
An Infinity of Mirrors - Ian Gouge, Coverstory books, 2018 (2nd ed.)
Losing Moby Dick and Other Stories - Ian Gouge, Coverstory books, 2017 (2nd ed.)
The Big Frog Theory - Ian Gouge, Coverstory books, 2018 (2nd ed.)

Short Stories

Degrees of Separation - Ian Gouge, Coverstory books, 2018
Secrets & Wisdom - Ian Gouge, Paperback, 2017

Poetry

The Myths of Native Trees - Ian Gouge, Coverstory books, 2020
A Kind of Making, Selected Poems 1979-2018 - Tom Furniss, Coverstory books, 2019
First-time Visions of Earth from Space - Ian Gouge, Coverstory books, 2019
After the Rehearsals - Ian Gouge, Coverstory books, 2018
Punctuations from History - Ian Gouge, Coverstory books, 2018
Human Archaeology - Ian Gouge, paperback, 2017
Collected Poems (1979-2016) - Ian Gouge, paperback, 2017

Anthologies

Oak Tree Alchemy - Ian Gouge, Coverstory books, 2019
Play for Three Hands - Tom Furniss, Ian Gouge, K.M.Miller, chapbook 1981

Plays

The Last Witch (2012), *First Light* (2015), *Seeing It Through* (2016), *The March* (2018) - Kate Miller, Pins & Feathers Productions
Circlemakers - Kate Miller, broadcast on BBC Radio Cambridgeshire, produced by Menagerie Theatre, Cambridge, 2010

Non-Fiction

Edmund Burke's Aesthetic Ideology: Language, Gender and Political Economy in Revolution - Tom Furniss, Cambridge University Press, 1993, 2008
Discovering the Footsteps of Time: Geological Travel Writing about Scotland 1700-1820 - Tom Furniss, Edinburgh University Press, 2018
Ways of Reading: Advanced Reading Skills for Students of English Literature - Tom Furniss (with Martin Montgomery, Sara Mills, Alan Durant, and Nigel Fabb), Routledge, 1992, 2000, 2007, 2012
Reading Poetry: An Introduction - Tom Furniss (with Michael Bath), Routledge, 1996, 2007, 2012

K M Miller
Ian Gouge
Tom Furniss

Triple Measures

With an Introduction
by Jason Best

First published in paperback format by
Coverstory books, 2020

ISBN 978-1-9993027-7-1

Copyright © K.M.Miller, Ian Gouge,
Tom Furniss and Jason Best 2020

The right of K.M.Miller, Ian Gouge, Tom Furniss and Jason Best to be identified as the authors of this work has been asserted by them in accordance with the Copyright, Designs and Patents Act 1988.

Cover image: "When Shall We Three Meet Again" © Monika Meisl Müller and reproduced with the gracious approval of the artist.

All rights reserved.

No part of this publication may be reproduced, circulated, stored in a system from which it can be retrieved, or transmitted in any form without the prior permission in writing of the publisher.

www.katemillerwriting.co.uk

www.iangouge.com

www.coverstorybooks.com

To our friends and tutors at Southampton
University, 1979-81

"When shall we three meet again?
In lightning, thunder, or in rain?"

from *Macbeth* (Act 1, Scene 1)
William Shakespeare

Contents

Foreword 3

First Measure: K M Miller

Botany 11
Cow Parsley 12
Eel Grass 13
Mountain 15
On Painswick Beacon 16
The Twelve Dancing Princesses 17
Murmuration 19
Fugue 21
Nought to sixteen weeks 22
New Year's Day 25
Feathers 26
Voices of Yellowstone 27

Second Measure: Ian Gouge

At 'Friar's Crag', Boxing Day, 2018 37
Railway Vignettes 38
Protest 40
Pilgrimage (#7) 42
Re-reading Larkin 43
Restoration 44
Letting Go 45
News 46
Hide 47
Curtain 48
Night Passage 49
A Candle, Guttered 50
Erosion 51
After the Concert 52
In Mourning (#9) 54
Grief 55
Vocal | Chords 56
from 'The Myths of Native Trees' 57

Third Measure: Tom Furniss

Road-kill Blackbird 65
St Boniface Down 67
Limes..68
Portrait in Black and White: For Ian Gouge 69
Blane Water 70
I Come Inside 71
Suffer Little Children..73
Trastevere..76
These Old Hands..79
Triple Measures 91

❃

Acknowledgements..93

Foreword

Kate Miller, Ian Gouge and Tom Furniss first came together as students just over forty years ago at the University of Southampton. There they collaborated in a writers' group run by the poet John Birtwhistle and were leading lights in the founding of an arts magazine for campus and city, The Definite Article. In their final year as undergraduates they again joined forces to publish a collection of their poetry, 'A Play for Three Hands'. Since then their careers and lives have taken divergent paths into different fields: Miller has become a freelance editor and playwright, Gouge an IT expert and novelist, and Furniss the author of several academic books on poetry, travel writing and philosophy. They continue, however, to share a love of and commitment to poetry.

Kate Miller

Flowers and birds. The subjects to which Kate Miller returns again and again in her verse couldn't be more quintessentially poetic. As topics go, they can be almost comically clichéd; the types of timeworn object a neophyte poet might reach for in her first stumbling efforts in verse.

Yet there is nothing the least bit hesitant or unfledged about Miller's poetry. It is deft, skilful, deceptively subtle. When she bestows attention on the natural world, the observations are exact and so is the language. 'Umbel', 'sepals', 'stamens', 'yarrow' and 'summer keck': these are the kinds of words and names she carefully alights upon. The precision, however, goes hand in hand with joyous appreciation.

'A love of flowers is a precious thing,' we find her declaring in 'Cow Parsley':

> A secret cache, a stash
> That's a jack-in-a-box of delight
> Leaping up at the touch of May.

'New Year's Day' contains this sharp-eyed, vividly sensual description:

> A kingfisher catches fire,
> Dousing its burnt copper belly
> In the muddy waters of the Ver.

Unlike the poet and her companion, however, not everyone is alert to such delight. The other people in the park, it seems, fix their gaze downwards rather than up. 'No one stops to see the other.'

It is a similar story in 'Voices of Yellowstone', where the park's visitors look without seeing; they 'gallop / From one gushing geyser / To the next gloopy mudboil.'

So observes the poem's 'Trickster Raven', one of a series of nature personifications who take turns in the poem to admonish us humans:

> Grasping smartphones and Gatorade
> You clock what you've come to see
> And glimpse nothing more.
> Box ticked. Check.

Our loss. Nature for Miller is nourishing, a replenishing bounty, a source of 'annual joy'. Yet this bounty is shrinking. Without resorting to polemic, she notes signs of ecological damage. In 'Eel Grass' a young and keen indigenous Canadian ecologist tells her on Vancouver Island that the old ways of marking the seasons are disappearing. 'The rhythms were being lost.' In 'Feathers' egrets arrive 'on the warm winds of climate change', while in 'Murmuration' starlings 'no longer turn city window-ledges black at dusk.'

> Our starved imaginations can't even dream
> Bison numerous as grains of sand,
> Or letting down a bucket in the sea
> To draw up glittering cod
> In abundance.

Miller's message is sobering, but there is nothing dour about her verse. It is tender, poised and alive with springy zest.

Ian Gouge

A vein of bruised romanticism runs through the poetry of Ian Gouge. Lost love, regret, grief and remembrance are themes to which he returns, yet surprising turns of phrase and turns of perception prevent his verse from becoming mournful or mawkish.

'At "Friar's Crag", Boxing Day, 2018' is typical in this regard. It describes a Lake District walk in which the poet and his companion come across the telltale signs of an ash scattering ceremony. The opening lines convey the rapid mental calibrations and revisions the poet makes in apprehending the scene, leading to a spry associative leap:

> we saw the flowers first
> tied hurriedly askew to a low fence
> less fence than coarse attempt
> to keep us to the rocky path
> the path from where we saw the dust
> not dust but pale grey ash
> less scattered than smuggled
> like a war-tunnel digger's
> tip and run under cover of night

In 'Alder', one of a series of wry, arboreal poems chosen from a larger sequence titled 'The Myths of Native Trees', a pair of furtive lovers meet with frustration after they leave a forest trail. There are hints of comedy in the mishaps that befall them, together with a note of rueful wisdom:

> away from the trail
> the heavy ground slowed our escape
> and later
>   mired ankle-deep in water

> we understood why some paths
> are seldom trodden

It isn't always the poet who is the butt of the joke, however. 'Protest' casts a gently humorous eye on the police:

> the uniformed looked on   passive
> as if nothing to do with them
> unconnected bystanders
> out for a stroll with their mates
> in Kevlar   just in case

Here, as elsewhere, Gouge favours the freest of free verse. Save for the sonnets 'Pilgrimage (#7)' and 'In Mourning (#9)', he largely avoids poetic forms freighted with literary history. Even so, the tug of tradition remains strong.

The ghost of Larkin hovers over several poems, a faint spectral presence in several, explicitly conjured up in another one. 'Railway Vignettes' softly echoes Larkin's 'The Whitsun Weddings'; 'Restoration' recalls his 'Church Going'; while 'Re-reading Larkin' is an amusingly narky meditation on the anxiety of influence that also conveys something of the shifts and slides in Larkin's reputation: costive librarian, literary great, dirty old man.

> All the while I can sense him
> looking over my shoulder
> as if marking my homework,
> a dubious figure in a grubby raincoat
> loitering at the back.

Tom Furniss

Tom Furniss takes great delight in craft. His poetry celebrates technique, artistry, true knack and know-how, whether it is the mastery of woodworking or of writing verse. Turning wood or turning phrases: both meet with his approval.

Unsurprisingly, he has a keen appreciation of poetry's nuts and bolts, paying close attention to rhyme, rhythm and metre. Also unsurprisingly, he has a keen appreciation of the writers who have gone before: 'the world's literature / circulates through me after a lifetime of reading,' he writes in 'Blane Water'.

Ballad forms are a particularly rich source, as in the poem 'Triple Measures', which rings and sings with a tripping, dance-like rhythm. Significantly, Furniss has also written verses expressly to be sung, and has previously collaborated with the Scottish composer Eddie McGuire on a number of songs and choral works.

Also harking back to ballads of old is 'St Boniface Down', a nimble, witty poem in which the writer looks back forty years to a visit with a past lover to the eponymous hill on the Isle of Wight:

> I'll meet you again on Boniface Down,
> We'll catch the shooting stars
> And watch as the moonlight crests the waves
> And the ferry boats head for France.

The poems 'Portrait in Black and White: For Ian Gouge' and 'Trastevere' also look longingly to a time forty years earlier, lamenting lapsed friendships and lost loves, as well as the loss of 'old-time skills' – in this case the art and craft of photography. Both poems revisit the mechanics of single reflex cameras and the chemistry of negative film, and the effort that went into mastering them:

> Changing aperture, adjusting
> Shutter speed, consulting
> The meter, checking depth of field,
> Fine-tuning focus with the slightest nudge
> Of the lens, all done at speed
>
> ('Portrait in Black and White: For Ian Gouge')

In 'Trastevere' a 10-line rush of tumbling enjambment briskly conveys what it is about the Roman street scene that compels the photographer to take a snap of his lover, but there's also a sense of anxious haste in his appraisal, which conveys the underlying tension between the pair:

> chiaroscuro, beautifully lit lines
> of those parked cars, that Beetle
> with the fold-down canvas roof
> you're walking past, stone steps
> worn by years of stepping out
> and stepping in, your shadow
> on the lit cobbles, old Roman
> shop signs, antique lamps lit
> by the feeble sun, shuttered
> windows

These poems share a tone that is both conversational and ruminative, qualities also found in the section's longest poem: 'These Old Hands'. Here we find personal recollections of the pursuits of childhood and fatherhood and times in between developing into a series of virtuoso riffs on hands in literature and art, culture and anthropology:

> Read it well: I've played my hand
> As best I could, tried all the tricks
> That poets use and critics like.

Jason Best, January 2020

First Measure: K M Miller

Botany

My cousin remarked
How the women of the family,
Examining an unfamiliar plant,
Rub the leaf,
And sniff.
Men don't do that, he said.

No. Too busy hunting
While we gather.

A woman will melt
Over her red Valentine roses,
Breathe in the scent
Of the bouquet beside her maternity bed,
Smile forgivingly
At the apology carnations with the price still on.

But deep down, as she gazes at the blooms,
The aeons-old question stirs in her:

Can I eat it?

Cow Parsley

Heart-deep in white flowers, he tries
To touch each umbel with his little finger
As we hurry along the hedgerow late for school.

You want your child to like what you like, and
A love of wild flowers is a precious thing.
A secret cache, a stash
That's a jack-in-a-box of delight
Leaping up at the touch of May.
An annual joy,
Forgotten in yellow August and grey January
To be rediscovered when you need it most.
Then you are swept up in the rush, the overspill
Of leaf and blossom:
Cow parsley, hawthorn, jack-in-the-hedge
Embellishing the lanes,
Bursting forth, reaching out,
Vying with each other, now now,
To fill the world with a froth of white
To the furthest edges of your vision.

The season passes; petals loosen.
But weeds pack seed-head, pod and fruit,
Filling their secret stores
For later, for another May,
For next year,
Another summer term.

Eel Grass

Vancouver Island

'Each plant has many meanings.'
He enumerated, eager that I understand.
'Ocean Spray. When its flowers turn brown
We know two things.
That the salmon will be plump.
And that it's time to hunt deer
For deer-fat.'
And when would it turn? I asked.
'It used to be late summer. But…'
He stopped. We both knew
The rhythms were being lost.

'And this one.' Yarrow, I recognised.
'Good for when a woman wants a baby.'
Another, unfamiliar plant:
'Good for when she doesn't.'

He was young and keen, an ecologist,
Working in this peaceful, popular inlet.
We looked out at the smart boats
Bobbing on the shallow tide,
Waiting for the weekend.

He said, 'This was my people's winter grounds.
It was ours, we'd always had the rights.
Then one day we came back from hunting
And they told us, you can't live here any more.
The land is needed for cement works.
So now we're all year in our summer place.'

He spoke as if it were last week.
But the cement works had long gone,
Their jetty crumbled and their lime leaching
Into the water.

'Eel grass,' he said.
'Cement, boat discharges, killed it off.
It grows deep under the water
And where there is eel grass
There are fish, insects, birds.

'This is our plan.' He smiled.
'To make the eel grass grow again.
It is laborious, we dive,
Every plant dug in the mud by hand
And weighted till it roots.'
A work of years.
He didn't seem to mind.

The sunlight flashed on the water
And I saw
What he saw:
The inlet flooded
With unseen life again.

Mountain

Five thousand feet up
Under a glacier
Whose advance and retreat
Has carved this valley
Of gravel and shale
Where little can grow,
Little can last,
Water seeps down to
An arctic blue pool,
A stream flows out
And at one place
A chance
Fissure in the rocks
Creates a creek
Where a seed has lodged.
A low willow grows
Its fallen leaves
Making a mulch
For other windfalls
To find a foothold,
Forming their own
Small green Eden.
In this – a white flower
Five green-veined petals
Five in-between sepals
Five bold stamens:
Parnassia palustris,
Grass of Parnassus,
The mountain of poetry
And music and dance.

On Painswick Beacon

Around our Guide camp the barley fields throbbed gold
In the rising heat under a high blue sky
We left the muggy canvas tents
The clatter of tin cooking pots and the smouldering fire
The dreams and discontent and midnight bitching
And were off –
Up the track, daps whitening in the dust
Girls laughing, unleashed
Past pale stone of boundary walls
Past green and white of summer keck and stitchwort
To the top of the hill, to the larks singing
High up, ever higher
To where we could stop running
And open ourselves to the wind.

The Twelve Dancing Princesses

The dancing princesses shuffle their feet
Going over the steps in their minds.
One will do a polka, one a rumba,
Others a gavotte, a quickstep, a bossa nova,
A strip-the-willow, a waltz, a jig,
A Sir Roger de Coverley, a pas de deux,
(On her own), a tango, a march.
They can barely move their face muscles
Under the makeup, their hair is tight
But their toes are twitching.

It's hard to be a princess
Living like this every night,
Hauling yourself out of bed
Exhausted in the morning,
Your mother shouting,
Another pair of shoes ruined.
The blue pearl shadow is running
Into the corners of their eyes,
The trembling lashes becoming unglued.
They cannot ask for help
From their competitor-sisters,
Cannot show weakness.
Every night they dance for their lives,
Not knowing if they will be chosen,
Not knowing if a missed step,
A hair out of place,
Will cost them the game.

One, the youngest, looks around,
She feels she is being watched.
A shadow slips behind a pillar.
But no time to think, never think.
Look, the boats are ready,
Each girl her own craft,
Taking her to dance her own dance
Alone
Up against the others, against the whole world.
Each one steps into a rocking boat
And points the prow to the magic ballroom.
Each knows she will succeed
If she can just believe in herself enough.

Murmuration

Like a single organism,
An amoeba,
An octopus,
A blob in a lava lamp,
A cloud of gnats,
A wave that turns into a loop that becomes a dart
That folds back on itself,

A flock of starlings skylark round West Pier.
In jittery, gleeful consensus they rise and wheel,
Dip to the sea foam and rise again,
Sticking close, never touching,
In a dance of controlled abandon.

Little posses join them,
Piling in from all along the coast
As the day dies.
They fly in high, then dive
Steep steep
To join the gang,
As the sun passes below the clouds
And gilds the wet pebbles.

Chattery, unloved starlings,
With their too-short tails
And mimic gift frittered away
On car alarms and trashy ring tones.
This small murmuration is a rarity:
They no longer turn city window-ledges black at dusk.
Nor are there winter fields covered

With plovers and redwings,
Telegraph wires sagging under swallows.
Our starved imaginations can't even dream
Bison numerous as grains of sand,
Or letting down a bucket in the sea
To draw up glittering cod
In abundance.

Some birds alight
On the skeleton of the pier and straight away
Take off, as if the iron ribs
Were burning hot.

The light turns leaden.
The flock is looser now.
Birds start to settle,
Furring the black girders
Like iron filings on a magnet.

As Brighton turns out
For another wild evening,
The starlings twitter, huddle, fidget,
Lift, turn, settle, chatter
Like annoying children.
Will they never go to sleep?

They fall silent.

Fugue

Four days after my brother's death
I found myself
In the Swan Hotel, Harrogate,
To which Agatha Christie fled,
Checking in, the second of February 1927,
Under her rival's name.

In the overheated bedroom,
Under peeling green paper,
I thought, 'He's dead'.
I slept. I woke
With the thought, 'He's dead'
Like a pillow over my face.

Who killed him?
Outside the wind howled with the voice
Of a family banshee, of a left-behind child.

I got up to investigate.
Bacteria swarmed in the cistern,
Accident lurked on the creaking stair.
I passed rooms where hearts were stopped, breath held.
I heard the tiny gunshot rattle of a typewriter.

Downstairs, in the darkened hallway,
Death was sulking. He beckoned me
To the oak-panelled door of the library.
Inside, Life, murder mistress of them all,
Was laughing.

Nought to sixteen weeks

Day 19
Beating the bounds of your new world,
We go down to the river,
Where coots scutter
And swans hold sway.

You have been here before:
Less than three days
Before you were born.
Now it is your father who carries you.
Do you recognise the paper rustle
Of the wind in the poplars?
Sense the silent flow
Of waters?

We walk, you sleep; you've safely made
The journey from watery cell,
To bed, to room, to river
And restless trees and bright, expanding sky.

Surveillance, weeks 6-8
You will be tested
(Not for the last time)
For startle reflex to sound,
Visual response,
Condition of the heart,
Testicular descent
And social smile.

But what about the secret smile
You give us, which delights
Beyond measure?

Eight weeks – growth
Small fists are smothered
By the sleeves of your three-to-six months suit.
You'll grow into it
And quickly.

You grow towards your gifts,
The human, the material:
The larger clothes waiting in the wardrobe,
Soft teddies, funny bunnies,
Things that dangle, rattle, squeak and shine
Which do not yet attract you.
Only bodies occupy you
Stomach, breast, arms.

We live in the present, each day bringing
A T-shirt tighter, a voice recognised
A new sound from your throat.

For days you did trial smiles,
Mirroring ours.
Some lopsided, some that took your face by surprise.
But now muscles stretch to make a smile
And you smile.
At eight weeks you have found delight.

What do you feel?
Hunger, cold, pain – we understand those.
But pleasure, do you feel it or do we
Merely read it?
Did you learn it
Or was it waiting within you?

Love – where does it come from?
Weak and ignorant, we make the gestures,
We try it on for size
And grow into it.

Night feed – 16 weeks
Somewhere there is a black cauldron
Into which time lobs our moments of love.
But from that generous brew
We can drink.
Lost moments like this one.
You've finished feeding now,
I press your soft scalp against my cheek.

You're half asleep; you'll grow
And have no memory of these times.
As I don't remember, but now know,
My mother fed me, night after night.

What is the use of all this love?
Children grow anyway and grow away.
But the cauldron bubbles.
I hope you'll drink from it.
One night when you hold someone in the dawn hours.

New Year's Day
G.M.H.

A kingfisher catches fire,
Dousing its burnt copper belly
In the muddy waters of the Ver.
Granting a vision of its glorious
Paradisaical blue.

We follow as it targets and drops,
Working the river from tree to tree,
Its eye and beak intent on fish.
Oblivious to those on the bank,
The not-fish, the other.

Look, look! I say and we watch
The bird do its timeless task
Of kingfisher
In peerless blue.

In the park, people walk.
Fixing their gaze on the path,
The pushchair, their partner.
Intent on new year resolutions,
Digging deep into their hearts,
Worrying away at their happiness, at
What I do is me.

Not one stops to see the other:
The kingfisher as he dives, splashes
And flashes, flashes again.

Feathers

Egrets have taken up residence
In the grounds of a former mansion house
Once fallen on hard times, the family
Constrained, the fortune
Dwindled, the stonework
Decayed.

Happily now redeveloped for discerning buyers,
Entrance and exit controlled
By electronic gates.

The egrets bypassed the security code
Arriving on the warm winds of climate change,
Spurning the French Riviera
For a season in the north.

In the heyday of the house, dances were held
Wheels crunched on the gravel, doors were opened
Ladies descended, curled and dyed plumes
Bobbing and swaying in their extravagant hats.

The egrets, pure white in the winter murk
Stand aloof, till they stab for a fish.

Downstream, their cousins, the big grey herons
Wait hunched, like brooding locals.

Voices of Yellowstone

Raven glides in to greet you.
Eyes, feathers, beak, talons
Black as the depths of hell.
Trickster Raven stands strong,
Feet firm upon the earth,
And opens the conversation.
Always the first word.
And the last.

Raven speaks
Welcome to the wonders,
The tease and the terrors
Of monstrous Mother Earth.
                Hey! What are you? The living dead?
                Listen up!
I get your gawps and gasps,
Your camera clicks and gallop
From one gushing geyser
To the next gloopy mudboil.
Grasping smartphones and Gatorade
You clock what you've come to see
And glimpse nothing more.
Box ticked. Check.

But you're in the caldera now.
The earth is more alive here
Than anywhere you know.
And to gain her harsh blessing,
You must be too.

Bison speaks

Here on this grassy plain of ease
I browse, I graze, I ruminate.
I slumber after lunch, I dream.
I doze by the road while cameras roll.

In a large, loose bunch we move,
Lumbering in front of cars.
You stop. We gaze. You wonder at us.
You feel our power.

Still, through our dark hides we fear.
We fear the wolves who eye our young,
But wolves pick one at a time.
We remember – you'd erase us all.

We remember your lust for land, for power
Satisfied only by mass destruction,
Your boiling greed spilling over,
Emptying prairies, scorching earth.

Sometimes, I wake gasping, crushed
Under the weight of slaughtered millions.
You let us roam here, assuaging your guilt.
It's a heavy burden to shoulder.

Old Faithful speaks
I perform like an elderly bear,
Chained and ragged with time.
Like the spout of a subterranean whale
Scarred from a thousand harpoons.
I am weary.

Every night I pray to the Mother,
The volcano in whose belly we sit:
Awake! Rise up from your slumber!
It is nearly your time again.
Break this thin crust of earth
And release me.

Wolf speaks
How long have we danced this waltz of death?
You advance, we retreat, you advance again,
Filling your firelight tales with our forms,
Though we are long gone from your days.

Yes keep picking away at the story
Of your heroic wars against us.
Clothe us in supernatural evil.
We remain the keepers of your dark longings.

The wolves were done for and the west was won,
This land made safe for stock and game,
The only creatures considered of worth.
Yellowstone secured and pacified.

Until the harmless elk came close
To destroying the weave. Balance had tipped.
Mild deer multiplied, devouring the green.
Pools clogged, creatures starved.

Now we wolves have restored order.
Headline predators of the national park.
You want to see us? You've never seen us,
Except through the night-scope of your fears.

How long till you learn not to eliminate all risk,
Learn to trust the unsafe?

Microbes speak
We are the first makers of this world,
Extremophiles thriving on hardship.
Scalding temperatures, zero oxygen, lakes of acid –
Bring 'em on!

We create colour and manufacture change.
In the ooze and steam and rotten egg stink
We swarm, perform our myriad roles.
We lap the shallow shores of rainbow pools,
Micro-forests of microbes forming a mat.
Some of us photosynthesise in the forest canopy,
Others work below in the liquid dark,
Bringing up our message from the underworld,
Expressed in fierce orange, red and violet.
Some of us gorge on the hydrogen sulphide
Lurking below. We create the acid
That eats rock and turns it to spewed mud.
As earth's innards come to the surface,
Released, gasping, from fumaroles and vents,

Meeting oxygen and sunlight, elements transform.
The magma only three miles under
Incubates us, cooks up combinations.
Thermophiles proliferate in earth's plumbing.
Our cousins thrive in the depths of the oceans,
Where volcanoes boil unseen in the blackness.
We were there at earth's earliest moves.
We might be multiplying on the moons of Jupiter,
Or waiting for you under the red crust of Mars.

Blue Gentian speaks
I bloom here at the brim of hell.
My blue stars catching the eye
Against the sulphur-yellow crust,
The bleached-grey scabbed ground.

How can I sustain life?
How can my Alpine-meadow innocence
Thrive, inhaling all the poisonous
Bad-breath of the underworld?

Follow me, seeker, into the earth.
Descend the fearful steps of your mind,
Let my blue torches light the path.
Adjust your eyes to the living dark.

Follow my roots as they stretch and sift
The nourishment from the toxic grime.
Feel me process darkness into colour.
Let my medicine show the way.

Raven speaks (again)

Welcome life in its many guises,
Where earth shows her workings.
Forget the norms and rules,
Where pools boil you alive,
Trees drink water that turns them,
Cell after cell, to stone.
Where out in the meadows and forest,
Creatures are born, are consumed.
Life works itself out
In ways you cannot grasp.

Cell after cell, life blooms
In the cauldron.

SECOND MEASURE: IAN GOUGE

At 'Friar's Crag', Boxing Day, 2018

we saw the flowers first
tied hurriedly askew to a low fence
less fence than coarse attempt
to keep us to the rocky path
the path from where we saw the dust
not dust but pale grey ash
less scattered than smuggled
like an escape-tunnel digger's
tip and run under cover of night
their loved one reunited with a favoured haunt
a place where now they lie
unprotected from the elements
they once embraced
to which they must finally succumb

they will be gone tomorrow
nothing left
but the flowers we saw first

Railway Vignettes

1
sheep lie in a field
there   a black one
another   and again
the rogue family of the estate

across the frosted hedgerow
the scar of a cavernous hole
a burial mound inverted
and silent diggers poised
in their uniform yellow
waiting for the day to start
like sheep in a field

2
the guard announces Burton-on-Trent
in bouncing sing-song
as if it's Torremolinos or some chart-topping destination
to which all your tracks have been leading

it isn't of course
but rather a nondescript place
with areas of posh and not
and huge brewery funnels
pumping the aroma of beer
into clean spring air

3
she limps as she walks
not because her trolley bag

black and trailing behind her
like a vaguely obedient dog
is especially heavy
nor because she is overweight (she is)
or her tights are laddered (they are)

she looks out of kilter
her hair uncombed   apologetic
as if it has already been a long day

she looks as if she wants
to be leaving   again
but she is just arriving
limping as she does

4
a woman sits with her son
and silently contemplates
the accidents of history
she wishes she could undo
as easily as slipping
a ring from a finger
as if that would free her
'til life us do part
free to go searching
for the things she lost
or the things she believes
have passed her by
like vignettes seen through
a railway carriage window

Protest

the banners were hand-made
crafted from garage leftovers
and worn out felt-tips   or their kids' ancient painting sets
letters shadowed in highlighter orange
        for emphasis   and fire
                colours running in the rain
they stole incendiary chants from the terraces
recycled   repurposed

the uniformed looked on   passive
as if nothing to do with them
unconnected bystanders
out for a stroll with their mates
in kevlar   just in case

in the drizzle some heads were hot
blinded by their cause
shackled by the impotence of their words

they shouted   their placards shouted
but no-one listened

an onlooker smoked languidly
and in a shop doorway a photographer
searched for an angle that would look perfect
in black-and-white
        waiting   in case it all kicked off

people moved slowly   or didn't move at all
tension taut like an elastic band
about   to   snap

a cry   the holding of breath
then from the back   an arm enflamed   swung

years later
the BBC voice-over has become legend
its words the narrative
        of the struggle
                the conflict
                        the outcome
and the black-and-white photo
of a uniform smeared with blood
        something motionless on the ground
                is a fable
                      or the only truth

the following weekend in bright sunlight
keepers in smart peaked caps   kits vibrant
the local derby a one-all draw
                        and the pubs all full again

Pilgrimage (#7)

We set-off before first light
the pre-dawn drive straining the eye.
Numbed by pulsing headlights, my sight
tried to race ahead, to preview the majesty
of the village beneath the hill,
a return to a bygone age
where all we knew and loved remained there still.
It was a pilgrimage
even if we struggled in the car
and travelling wasted too much of the day.
"That's just the way things are"
you said. We were about halfway,
stopping for lunch at noon
already resigned to return too soon.

Re-reading Larkin

All the while I can sense him
looking over my shoulder
as if marking my homework,
a dubious figure in a grubby raincoat
loitering at the back.
Is that expression the resentment
he has to loiter there at all
or merely suburban anger at time
wasted on me?

Annoyed at the intrusion
he tuts under his breath
as he might a noisy bookworm.

'How many more fucking times
do I need to tell you?'

Waving a stubby pencil at a half-rhyme
he shakes his head
then shoulders his camera
determined to capture more of this miserable life
before it gets too late.

Left alone,
I weigh-up the merits of pairing
'blarney' with 'money'
and ask myself why *I* like to go into churches.

Restoration

scaffolding surrounds the church
ribs skeletal about the tower
its skin of rough tarpaulin hints
at Norman regularity and hidden fractures
        a cracked lintel
        gargoyles weather-worn
        glass more shattered than stained

inside
darkness triumphs over feeble candles
no matter how many are remembered
and where light should paint
rainbow shafts against memorial walls
nothing but a ghostly residue
like a confession's resonance
veneered against the curtained stall

memory whispers in the echo of your footfall
prompted too by damp stone and old oak pews
recalls school excursions with crayons and paper
searching for brasses upon which
to overlay an infant skill

out in the wind again
the loosely wrapped tarpaulin flaps
like Christmas paper slack around presents
you knew you were getting
        or emptily
        like all those hollow promises
        which remain unfulfilled

Letting Go

an entrance through rough scrub
leads to unmapped landfill
poorly disguised behind forlorn hedgerows
scant welcoming for birds

rutted tracks betray the trespassers
who come in darkness
to divest themselves of the unwanted
sloughing off flakes of veneer
as if they were snakes shedding skin

my car steers erratically
its narrow wheelbase a mismatch
for deep and puddled ruts
skimming the mud's crust
its chassis gouging my progress
like a tell-tale tracing
on a well-worn map

parked beside a buckled mattress
I unload today's modest offering
    part-read classics
      the corpse of an unkept diary
      a notebook whose last few naked pages
        seem beyond salvation

tossing them into the blackness
should feel like a release
but they are greeted by silence
like sacrifices looking for a cause

News

I wait for the telephone to ring.
The inevitability of it.
This is a strange waiting,
a long waiting
              wishing for something not to happen
    even though it must.

I tried your line today.
My turn to call.
There was nothing after the dialling tone
as if that was the end of it,
                    nothing more
                            nothing left.
For a moment it was liberating.

Hide

Sleuth-like you scavenge for clues:
the roughness of bark to the touch,
a musky odour you can smell in the fog.

You imagine a slender, mouse-grey bird
and strive to describe it given only
the nocturnal song of one of its neighbours.

Undaunted, there is no option but
to go deeper in on a close summer night,
embracing a legend worth believing.

Absorbed in a cocoon of quiet industry
you find him watching and waiting,
perched in the blind, silently writing.

Curtain

between the valley and the peak
fragments of light sliding through the clouds
flicker like scraps of confetti
easily slipped into stillness

breathing hard through an open smile
his eyes see with specific literacy
ancient waterfalls carving in slow motion
a ribbon of majestic beauty
one side of a mortal veil
drifting like a cobweb in the air

Night Passage

Flitting addictively between emotions
quiet imbalance has become an epidemic
a foil for the prescription used to manage life.
You search for medication to settle
the nervous twitch that turns recording into editing,
cements experience into long-term memories,
dusty volumes logged in a Dewey catalogue.

Once you believed in the ancient craft
and tried stitching a robe from haphazard scraps,
a gift as rare as a handwritten letter.
Exhausted by the effort, you find history
is a serpentine descent into an alternative world
rewarded by snatched dreams
where sometimes we believe we can fly.

All too late you discover sleep is a gift
denied to the insomniac and the guilty,
defined by something it is not.

A Candle, Guttered

betrayed by this soft groove
a fountainhead melted in hot light
its bequest   an uneven trail
pale witness of lives
traded for a compendium of importance
or of trivia   perhaps

did we realise
or were we seduced by such moments
our testimonies compiled from fragments
like a seed-cloud
airborne in a ripe dandelion field

perhaps one seed settled
        here   or here
an idea given the chance to root
and begin the cycle again

perhaps   in the candlelight
we talked about dandelions
and what weeds were
no more   you said   than ideas growing
where they were not wanted

I thought of our past
and what had separated us
and how a guttered candle
might tell the story

Erosion

the pebbled beach
a congregation celebrating
the tribulation of tides
smoothed to impossible ellipses
that beg to be spun back out to sea
as if relaunched into their past

and I wonder how the tides have worked on you
corrupting your once unblemished surface
each wave-clash sending blade-sharp shards
dangerous through the air

what was it shaped you
to become the dark flint
firing sparks from our past

After the Concert

falling foul of memory's snare
the fragile recollection
of an evening when time crept
so slowly
it felt as if we owned it
as if the moon
would never break beyond the branches
of that winter ash

it was romantic I suppose
but I
confused
was torn between longings
for time to crawl
so that I could hold you there
for time to race
that I might hold you breathless elsewhere

lately it is not time I recall
but the chill of the night
the cold of the fire-escape rail
on my empty hands
the dull thumping from the concert hall
the tremolo of my heart

in prescient mood
even then I knew what would come
later that night
and the next when you gently let me down

the moon passes beyond the ash
illumination of a fragment of time
the varnish and shadow
of a passing moment

In Mourning (#9)

There used to be a sparkle in your eye
fired by a vigorous joust with life.
I watched it die
as I watched you lose your wife,
so desperate to weep
yet dry-eyed at being left behind.

She would have told you what to do: to keep
focused on the future,   your mind
alive,   sharply honed on how to spend
your time,   not waste it
as she feared she had at the end.

You say I cannot understand it,
how heavily it sits,
not death but the emptiness it commits.

Grief

there is a space where you used to be

I see it on grey station platforms
and in shuffling supermarket aisles

strange how it is never occupied
                                 despite the throng

I feel it during countryside walks
my hand abandoned
constantly surprised to find yours
                                 not there

a voice   lost like me   asks
not why you are not here
                       but why am I

and why do I bother to make that journey
        or go to work
               or read this book

they say all stories have two sides

if that is true
then I am living half of ours
staring at the space you once filled

Vocal | Chords

I want a voice of my own. | A rasp like Dylan's -| two bars, you know it's him. | A voice is not what you say | but how you say it; | Dylan could wring agonies | from Mary and her little lamb. | If you spoke another language | you could still tell it was Dylan | or Sinatra. | Or Betjeman, come to that. | A voice exists beyond the words, | in the insubstantial spaces between them, | living the high-life in a parallel universe. | So I weave words on the page | to create a portal to another realm, | to connect to a sense beyond the surface, | braving all the self-scrutiny | to summon up the courage | to see if I can get there.

from 'The Myths of Native Trees'

Alder

in a forest   green is no camouflage

we sought refuge
              concealment
mistaken in our naïve belief
hiding beneath the alders' canopy
      our secret
             our elopement
would remain hidden

away from the trail
the heavy ground slowed our escape
and later
      mired ankle-deep in water
we understood why some paths
                     are seldom trodden

in a forest   green is no camouflage

Ash

"My passion is animals" you said
        your voice in the mid-distance
            off-hand
        as if it belonged somewhere else
            to someone else

"The serpent and the eagle" you said
        after I queried your favourites
"They are full of insight and wisdom"
        your voice betraying a longing
            for something mystical or magical
            of another place

"Did you know" you said
"from the antlers of a deer
sprang the rivers of the world?
That the serpent and the eagle
protect the purity of springs?"

        I was always confused in your world
            as if it were not my home

"You belong in the underworld" you nearly said
        watching me as I fashioned
        spears from the bough of an ash
            then concentrating
                took aim

Birch

furred by freezing fog
the landscape waits nervously
for the emergence of spring
as if it were a promise
never guaranteed

sitting in an attic bedsit
he reads about witches
and how broomsticks are made
as if both were real
he reads about potential
about love and renewal
and dreams of goddesses who might rescue him
driving out the daemons
who feed on winter solitude

in the sky
the moon lingers
elbowing its way into the day
as if to prove a point

we give it names
in recognition of its importance
and our subservience
        blood
                blue
                        wolf
                                worm
but never spring

Cherry

in the tree
the cuckoo watches
as the bough
              bends
with a force it never knew it had
to kiss the hand of a woman
heavy with her own fruit

the bird has no song for this
and feels
        for the first time
an interloper

silently it unfurls its feathers
and moves on

Third Measure: Tom Furniss

Road-kill Blackbird

My son brought home
A dead blackbird,
Someone else's road-kill,
Picked up against his mother's will
Carefully in gloves,
Brought home without a trace
Of sentiment so we
Could make a meal of it.
Sunken eyes would never learn to see
Or broken wings fly
Again, never more arise
Into a blue February sky
Like today's, or sing
From the crown of the holly tree
Late into the night.
I'd already begun to cook
Tonight's spaghetti bolognaise.
He finally agreed to bury it
Under the slab of Aberfoyle slate,
Our garden's standing stone,
That looked like a gravestone waiting
For a corpse; he drove a stake
Into the earth to mark the spot
And wanted to make a cross.
He said he believes in God.
He loaded the bird-feeder
Hanging on the holly tree
With sunflower seeds
Not to help birds through winter frosts
But to lure them into the garden

So he might shoot them with his bow
And deadly sucker-tipped arrows.
Hunting with a bow is a story
Boys inhabit to become themselves.
A hundred thousand years,
Generations of men
Taking boys to hunt for food, survival,
Have shaped his DNA for this.
Christianity's a recent mutation.
Romantic poetry unread as yet.

St Boniface Down

I'll meet you again on Boniface Down,
We'll catch the shooting stars
And watch as the moonlight crests the waves
And the ferry boats head for France.

I'll meet you there on the longest day
At midnight on the heights
Where we made love an age ago
On the long hot summer nights

We'll wake the constellations again
And the saint from his unknown grave
We'll search once more for the wishing well
And the beaches where we bathed

We'll drink anew from the sacred spring
Forget the years between
Make love once more on the yielding grass
Allow ourselves to dream

Yet this is just a song I made
And songs are rarely true
Five hundred miles and forty years
Remain between us two.

Limes

Lime trees embower poets whom
We never more may see again,
Lime cliffs embrace fossils
Of long dead creatures
We might never have seen
Given the brief span of our lives
If salt-seas didn't storm beaches
Or frosts find cracks in cliffs
And bring them down bones and all
For hammer-tapping naturalists
To discover, examine, compare,
Gradually come to earth-
Shattering conclusions
About creation, preservation,
Destruction, age of the earth,
Eventual fate of all
That we hold dear, very ground
We stand on. I read
That poet's words again,
Penned a mere two hundred years
Ago, who never could accept
What those rendered bones reveal,
Or see that poetry holds out
Against the loss of time
Only until the last remnants
Of humanity
Have been folded into sea-stormed cliffs
And cast on an empty beach
For no one to read.

Portrait in Black and White: For Ian Gouge

You've walked back into the picture now
I've finally realised the light
Cannot be measured after forty years;
In the interim, camera phones and internet
Have jammed our lives
With billions of photographs
Perfect and instantly redundant
And done away with the need to think
About the physics of light
And how the mechanical engineering
Of single reflex cameras used to control
Exposure, and we've lost those old-time skills
We tried so hard to master –
Changing aperture, adjusting
Shutter speed, consulting
The meter, checking depth of field,
Fine-tuning focus with the slightest nudge
Of the lens, all done at speed
To capture a moment of now
That we'd never see again
And that usually passed us by
In the flick of an eye. I loved
That old Russian Zenith
Found second-hand (at least)
In an old camera shop – heavy metal,
Wholly manual, flickering needle
For a meter, slow to use.
There was a moment on that memorable day
In Oxford all those years ago
I missed: you walked out of the picture
Without knowing it, while I struggled
To measure the light.

Blane Water

It's almost certain some of the molecules
Of H^2O now mingling in the waters
Of the Blane flowing under the bridge
At the bottom of our road once jostled in
The river outside Troy that almost drowned
Achilles; even more likely that this river
Which follows my daily walk is partly composed
Of water from that flood which drowned the world
For the sins of men in ancient myth, and later
Flowed through the river pool in which John dipped
The son of man; and some of it must have tumbled
Out of the highest mountains in the world
And lost itself in the Ganges many times
To purify the bodies of the dead,
Releasing souls from endless rounds of birth
And death; hydrologic cycles have gyred
The planet's water since it first appeared on earth
Perhaps from outer space; here inner space
Can be explored watching the river flow
Where writings of the world can circulate
And it's worth knowing just downstream from here
The village sewage works distils pure water
From our excremental waste and pumps
It in the Blane; we are excreting bodies
Not just souls yet poetry flows on
In a million channels endlessly recycling
Images from Iliad, from Gita,
And the ancient dreams of Israel.

I Come Inside

I'll never come again
In you or anyone else,
In my hand or in my dreams
Or in somebody's mouth.

I wore a catheter for fourteen weeks
Then had my prostate reemed
By a skilled surgeon on the NHS;
My pee now freely flows
Under my control;
A surgical strike
With little collateral damage –
Neither rendered impotent
Nor yet incontinent.

But now I come inside
Myself, back-firing,
Retrograde ejaculation;
It's on the list
Of possible side effects.

No more eruptions, mighty fountains,
The tide has turned forever,
The river runs back
Towards its source,
The old geyser (geezer?) spurts
In hidden caverns
Measureless to man,
Faithful no more.

I come into my inner self, secrete
Myself in secret, no expense
Of spirit in a waste of shame.

Like those adepts of Taoist sex
I treasure my vital fluid,
My Jing;
They think it travels up the spine
To nourish the brain, preventing
Premature aging.

My newly-nourished brain knows
That's a myth, of course.

It might come, my GP said,
With emotional difficulties.
Come, come, I say. I'm too old now
For that kind of thing.

Of more interest to me
Are those internal spontaneous overflows
Of upwelling lava
We call poems.

And I'm thankful that
My only begotten son
Was born seven years before
The source was dammed.

Suffer Little Children

Suffer little children, Jesus said,
in Matthew, Mark and Luke,
but not in John, forbid them
not to come unto me:
for such is the kingdom of heaven.
Not, as some Christians seem to think,
or thought not long ago: let them suffer
(it's good for them and they deserve it,
being born in sin), but just the opposite –
allow them, let them come to me so
I can cure their suffering through my own
or glimpse heaven in their play.
This is not the only biblical use
of 'suffer' in this sense, yet
some who claim they've taken up his cross,
would straighten out his verbal play,
replace his poetry with words
that make plain modern sense:
'Let the little children come to me'.
That's plain enough, but where's
the miracle of meaning? I doubt
he coined new words and meanings
on the spot, he needed water
for the wine, but loved a pun
(founding his church on a rock)
and 'suffer' neatly conjures
images of suffering
even as it cancels them.
Yet Jesus didn't speak English, of course,
not even that of Shakespeare's time.

The Gospels were written in Greek.
Let's check the word on the internet:
Αϕετε from *aphiemi*, to permit.
The link with suffering is not yet there.
'Suffer' first appeared in Tyndale's Testament,
for which he suffered death in 1536
on the orders of a king,
for suffering children who drive the plough
to know their scriptures better
than their betters. He never knew
that most of his marvellous poetry,
copied by those authorised scribes
hired to translate this troublesome book
so it wouldn't foster revolution,
would inspire readers and poets across the globe
for centuries to come. Yet Jesus spoke
not Greek but Aramaic, everyday
demotic in Judea at that time.
What word did he use? Was it as good
as 'suffer'? We'll never know
or even if he lived at all.
We only have the words of those evangelists,
who wrote about a man who suffered
on a cross before their time
and never wrote a word himself.
That they more-or-less agree on what he said
nothing proves. They made
three versions of a character
(four with John's) and put some lofty
speeches in his mouth (and some that puzzle still),
at least in Tyndale's English,
inspiring poetry if not belief.
Was something gained in translation,

only to be lost once more
in those new improved translations
no one but believers care to read?
In the end, I'm glad to say,
we still can read the poetry
that should challenge us to end
the suffering of the children of the world
that goes on day by day, two thousand years
after Jesus' suffering on the cross
was meant to end it all,
washed up on beaches, drowned
in rivers, exploited on the internet,
abused by scribes and Pharisees
who claim to lead them unto Christ
(who wouldn't cover up their crimes
but hang a millstone round their necks
and drown them in the depths of the sea).
We can't wait for him to come again –
despite the double meaning of those words.

Trastevere

Here's a photograph of you
walking the cobbled back streets of Trastevere
in the winter of eighty-three
or thereabouts, thin light glancing
off rain-varnished *sampietrini*
polished smooth by the centuries;
you're walking in the footsteps of so many
who have passed this way and passed away,
most of whom were never caught
in a moment like this, pushing
black and white film to its limit –
cold white of the sky above buildings
grey with various shades of age,
impenetrable film noir shadow of that stylish
boot-length coat, your ghostly face
barely emerging out of the gloom
like the features of the Turin Shroud
more imagined than seen
lovely and tilted like a Leonardo sketch
I loved before I ever fell in love with you;
I worked hard alone in the darkroom
to bring out your face, made many test strips,
varied the developing time again and again
but never got it clearer than this print
and only now I see how right it is,
moving all-the-more for being barely there,
summing up and summoning
that drunken rain-swept winter day in Rome
when hand in hand we walked the streets
not knowing what had come between us,

and all that red red wine
just made it worse; all roads led us
to that street, moment, photograph:
you, poised, not posed, mid-step in silhouette,
hands in pockets, shoulders hunched,
wild hair depressed by the rain, shadowed
face giving nothing away, almost nothing
to the camera, barely light enough
to spark the chemistry of the film,
yet saying everything about that day
we lost ourselves
in the backstreets of Trastevere;
what was it that urged me to take that shot,
so much against your will –
chiaroscuro, beautifully lit lines
of those parked cars, that Beetle
with the fold-down canvas roof
you're walking past, stone steps
worn by years of stepping out
and stepping in, your shadow
on the lit cobbles, old Roman
shop signs, antique lamps lit
by the feeble sun, shuttered
windows? – all of that I think,
and there's no denying
that the composition's good,
the tone and atmosphere just right;
I remember trying to emulate
Henri Cartier-Bresson's photos,
but for me now it represents
impossibility – of making time
stand still, however fast
the shutter speed, however old

the streets we wander, however eternal
the city – and the fallacy
that photographic film might fix
love, another human being, or me.

These Old Hands

('Well, well; I heard Ahab mutter, "Here some one thrust these cards into these old hands of mine; swears that I must play them, and no others"' (Herman Melville, *Moby Dick*, chapter 118).)

    1

An old hand is a veteran,
Experienced, adept, and skilled,
A dab hand at his craft, or hers,
Whose old hands know their trade;
I've turned my hands to various arts –
Gardening, hiking, sports and games –
That I've pursued for many years,
And I'm handy enough at working wood,
And hands have played an unsung part
In reading, teaching, writing poems
More than half my life; we take
Old hands for granted, as I mine,
They get on with their tasks with quiet
Unobtrusive skill and tact,
But now I'll take a second look
With the fresh eyes of an old hand.

    2

Look at these old hands of mine,
Still warm and capable despite
Their more than sixty years of use,
Skin brown and rough and wrinkled with
Time and play, work and sun,
Setting off a golden wedding ring,
A flattened nail right next to it
Stepped on in a schoolboy scuffle

Fifty years ago, and thin white
Scars on the left hand's pointing finger
That mark the wounds I gave myself
Learning to use my first penknife,
Making penny whistles, cutting
My initials in the bark of trees,
Whittling in the woods and fields
I came to know like the back of my hand

These hands I hold before you now
Will be sixty-seven next early spring;
Hands that have done so many things
From the time before my memory
To the typing of these lines; I must
Have grasped and held my mother's hand
When she was all-in-all to me,
But have no recollection now;
From early on there were tools to hand –
Pencils, pens, brushes, knives –
To draw and write, paint and carve,
And my hands were into everything –
Stroked dogs and cats and fed the hens
Cleaned out rabbits and skinned them when
Their time had come; my mother taught
My hands to plait a rope from strands
Of baling string from the farmer's barn
And how to shuffle and deal out hands
Of whist and how my hands should hold
My cards and how to play the hand
I'm given, and how to light a fire –
My father taught me outdoor skills
Like splitting kindling, chopping wood –
But they found themselves the way to steal

Forbidden fruit from neighbours' plots –
Like poaching, scrumping was an art
Practised in earnest by country boys –
To bowl and field red leather balls,
Play all the strokes with willow bats,
Climb swaying trees, make catapults,
And how to cast a line, disgorge
A hook from the mouths of fish, pick
Rose-hips, mushrooms, blackberries,
And new potatoes fresh from the earth;
Once formed a fist and bloodied the nose
Of one of my mates on the school bus
When argument got out of hand,
Carefully handled 12-inch discs
And lowered pickups onto grooves,
Practised dealing by sleight of hand,
Tortured fingers fretting guitars
And tortured the songs I loved the most,
And turned the leaves of many books,
Adopted the mudras of meditation,
Sought to grasp the sound of one
Hand clapping in my silent soul,
Wrote a careful hand with a scratchy nib
In primary school and won first prize
For handwriting in 'sixty-four,
And poetry on laptops now.

These hands have played and worked in earth
From earliest times and handled spades
And forks and hoes, and used the toys
And tools that made humanity
And made my world: woodland dens
With knives and knotted baling string,

Catapults from forks in trees,
Trucks from planks and wheels of prams,
Lathe and drill, saw and plane,
Mallet and chisel, clamp and vice,
And still I love to work these tools
And love the tools themselves.

I've crewed a yacht (all hands on deck),
Worked briefly as a factory hand,
Cooked for friends and lovers, wife
And child, consoled those friends whose pain
And loss seemed keener than my own,
Held many a pint and joint and learned
To roll them in my mad-cap days.

I was seventeen when first I felt
The electric touch of a girlfriend's hand
Like the hand of God reaching out
For Adam's hand on the Sistine ceiling
About to give the spark of life
To all humanity; since then
These hands I look at now have held
Many women in acts of love,
Gave pleasure I hope, explored the sweets
And secrets of their bodies and loved
Myself as well.

These old hands are still quite apt
To learn new tricks and skills and games;
Dry stone walls in need of repair,
Another kind of outdoor game,
Slabs to lay for a garden shed,
A pond to dig and wood to cut

With chainsaw never used before
And store for winter fires, and teach
My son, already handier
Than any child I've ever known,
To use the hand- and power-tools
His inner self compels him to,
Make pinky promises with him
That never can be broken.

    3

Letting go is harder to learn
For grasping hands than holding on,
But we needed both for our life in trees,
And for our latest being, doing –
I needed the art of letting go
For throwing stones and cricket balls,
Releasing arrows when the bow is bent
And letting go of lovers' hands
When love had gone before, but I
Held fast to mother's hand as she
Slipped away from me to death.

    4

There's a grotesque creature you need to see,
A sensory homunculus
Whose limbs and organs are re-sized
According to their sense of touch –
Enormous tongue and lips and hands
Grafted on a puny body,
Monstrous image of how we sense
The outer world and inner self,
Massive hands ready to clasp
The world in a giant's embrace.

5

Articulate hands have their own know-how,
Are tools of consciousness that help
The mind to grasp itself and all
The world besides. And when I touch
That stone or stroke the touchpad or
These laptop keys I feel the hand
That's feeling them and sense myself
More deeply still when one hand holds
The other or itself; these hands
Touch me, I feel for them, they hand
Me to the world and are the world,
All the world, to me.

6

Hands are old in human years
But young in terms of life on earth,
Began their long evolution from
The pectoral fin of fish; prehensile
Primates' hands and feet evolved
From tree shrews sixty million
Years ago; the human hand
Emerged with us from forests and trees
When hands were freed for making tools
And making tools changed hands and minds
Two million years ago and made
Our species different to the rest
And pushed the brain on its forward path
And gave our kind the upper hand,
And let us tell ourselves that God
Gave us dominion.

7

Quintilian said that hands can play
Their part in the art of rhetoric;
They make a language of their own,
Gestures we barely notice, signs
And symptoms of the speaking body,
Shake hands and wave goodbye hello,
Make obscene gestures, friendly signs,
Thumbs up, thumbs down, two different Vs,
Show friends what we mean as we talk on the phone,
And sign the manual languages
Of those who cannot hear.

They are also highly numerate:
Let's count the bones that make a hand:
Twelve phalanges in four fingers,
Two in each of the thumbs, and five
Metacarpals in the palm,
Eight carpals in the flexing wrist;
Children learn to count on hands:
Ten digits on two hands allow
Counting in tens to seem the norm,
Twelve phalanges on four fingers
(Touchable by thumbs) gave rise
To dozens of other counting systems
Across the world way back in time.

8

The left hand knows what the right is doing,
In every task, at work or play,
There's nothing sinister or gauche,
Unlucky or impure in the left,
Divine, benign or especially clean

About the right – they wash each other,
Do different kinds of task, combine
In arts and crafts, sports and love;
The right arm happened to be the arm
That early humans used to throw,
Handed down from father to son
And carried now in our DNA,
So the right hand seems to be the one
For fighting, writing and all those arts
Of the hand we think distinguish us
From animals, our lower selves;
But bend a bow and tell me then
If the hand that draws the string to your ear
Has a nobler task than the one that keeps
The straining bow at the length of your arm
Steady and true; and bowing a Strad
Without the left hand's fingering
Would make a sorry tune; the left
Hand brings the fork to the mouth and holds
The wood for the saw, the flint to be chipped;
Would the right hand's melody still touch
Our hearts without the harmony
Of the left hand's chords?

9

Do these fortune-teller's flexure lines –
Heart line, head line, fate line, Sun line,
Girdle of Venus and the rest –
Crossing palms like dried up river
Beds, really tell my fate
And character? do I truly hold
The future in my hands? These patterns
Of minute ridges on my finger

Tips – these friction pads, which help
With grasping branches upside down
And swiping mobile phones – remain
Unchanged throughout a life of change,
Unique to me among the teeming
Billions of hands on earth,
Identity persisting through
Complete replacement of the cells
Every seven years

      10

Hands are strewn throughout our speech
In metaphors and idioms;
And play their parts in old texts too:
Old Testament hands are instruments
Of a jealous and a wrathful God,
Made in the image of those who made
Him up, and used for violence;
There's reason to fear when a hand appears
In that dreadful holy text: the earth
Opened its mouth to drink his brother's
Blood from the hand of Cain, and every
Creature of the earth is given
To the hand of Noah for the meat of men;
And hands take knives to animals' throats
Repeatedly to appease their God;
Abraham was ready to lay hand on his son
As sacrifice to his awful Lord,
The wild man's hand is turned against
Every man, and every hand
Is turned against him; the vengeful Lord
Frees the chosen with a mighty hand,
And strikes them for their sins in turn,

Smites his people and their foes
Over and over, obsessively,
Lets Moses curse idolaters
With outstretched hand and gives him power
To part the sea by a wave of the hand
And close it again to overwhelm
The Egyptian host their enemy
(We don't count the dead when God's on our side);
The words God spoke through Moses' hand
Strike horror in our humane hearts
And the tablets of stone are dipped in blood:
No chance of pity in an eye for an eye,
A tooth for a tooth, a hand for a hand;
And the stones in the hands of the righteous mob
Are put there by the hand of God.

Sickened by this it's relief to turn
To the Gospel stories of Jesus Christ
Which gradually replace the laws
Of Moses with the law of love,
Where the kingdom of heaven is nigh at hand
And God is done with smiting and
The cutting off of offending hands
Is a metaphor and Jesus' hands
Heal withered hands and cure the sick
And raise the dead and break bread
And wash apostles' feet; when scribes
And pharisees would stone a woman
Taken in adultery
He made the righteous drop the stones,
From guilty hands and slink away,
Forgave the woman and thereby broke
The temple law; a multitude

Laid their hands on him, priests and servants
Smote him with the palms of their hands
And soldiers nailed him to the cross
By his healing hands.

In Shakespeare's plays there's blood on hands
And hands are treacherous instruments
Wielding death to queens and kings
And enemies of kings as well,
Clutch daggers serving death to guests,
And bathe themselves in Caesar's blood,
And all great Neptune's ocean can't
Wash guilty blood from guilty hands
Which never will be clean again;
Even when star-crossed lovers' hands
Do touch as pilgrims touch saints' hands
It leads them to the tomb and death
At their own hands.

11

I look at you now, old hands, as if
For the first time in my life; I've never
Thought so much about you two,
Partners in crime, in work and play,
Each other's helping hands and mine,
Who've worked for me my whole long life,
Who take or make the things I need
And make me what I am, or dwelt
On the role of hands as human beings
Emerged from evolution,
Or read our founding texts with hands
In mind or saw the hand that hands
Have played in everything I love

And much of what I hate; this poem
Has made you, hands, quite strange to me,
And made you my familiars
Again.

    12

This poem is at an end at last,
Its fate is in the hands of you
Who hold and read it now, dear reader;
Read it well: I've played my hand
As best I could, tried all the tricks
That poets use and critics like;
Old hands will spot allusions or
Identify the metre and
Compare it to the better poems
They've read throughout their reading lives;
New apprentice hands may doubt
That hands can form a poem without
Spontaneous overflowing feelings;
I only hope this hand I hold
Towards you now will make you look
With new eyes at your own old hands
And all the things they do.

Triple Measures

I'll have three triple measures of triple new pleasures,
Fill all these tumblers with gold,
Our spirits are high but let's spirit them higher,
So pour out those measures of old.

I don't care if the law won't permit triple measures,
Let's stoke up our bellies with fire,
Don't allow lousy lawyers to limit our pleasures,
The landlord is worthy his hire.

Not one no nor two only three triple measures
Will lead us to treasures tonight,
Come my two darlings let's triple our pleasures
Let's romp in the pale blue moonlight.

Let's go early to bed, I'll be early to rise,
We'll ride our white steeds 'till the morn,
We'll take it quite slowly but end with a gallop,
And we'll dance triple measures at dawn.

*

Acknowledgements

We are grateful to Monika Meisl Müller for permission to use her wonderful piece "When Shall We Three Meet Again" on our cover, and to Charlotte Hurrell for facilitating that agreement.

Previous publications:

- "Pilgrimage" was first published in the online edition of 'The Aesthetic Apostle', February 2019
- "Alder", "Ash", "Birch", Cherry", "At 'Friar's Crag', Boxing Day, 2018", "Railway Vignettes", "Protest", "Re-reading Larkin", "Restoration", "Letting Go", "News", "Hide", "Curtain", "Night Passage", "A Candle, Guttered", "Erosion", "After the Concert", "Grief" and "Vocal I Chords" are also published in *The Myths of Native Trees*, by Ian Gouge, Coverstory books, 2020
- Versions of "At Friar's Crag, Boxing Day, 2018", "Vocal I Chords", "Curtain", "Cherry", "In Mourning", "Protest", "Grief", "A Candle, Guttered" were first published on www.writeral.com

www.ingramcontent.com/pod-product-compliance
Lightning Source LLC
Chambersburg PA
CBHW060405080526
44583CB00012B/481